FREI

New and Selected Poems

Shearsman Books
Exeter

Published in the United Kingdom in 2006 by
Shearsman Books Ltd
58 Velwell Road
Exeter EX4 4LD

ISBN-13   978-0-907562-98-6

ISBN-10   0-907562-98-1

Acknowledgements
New Poems:
Acumen, London Magazine, Poetry Salzburg

Older Work:
My thanks to those who published me, notably (but not exclusively):
Xenia Press (Peter and Ginny Barnfield), Circle in the Square (Bill
Pickard), Lomond Press (R.L. Cook), *Outposts Magazine* (Roland John),
Northern House (Jon Silkin), *Acumen* (Patricia Oxley), Etruscan Books
(Nicholas Johnson), and Menard Press (Tony Rudolf). An especial thanks
to the late Jon Silkin and *Stand*, who supported me for a quarter of a
century, and Dr James Hogg of Salzburg University Press who issued
three volumes of my poetry, besides an anthology and a work of prose
criticism. It is doubtful if these poems would have been written but for
the support of various friends, notably: Hazel Beale, Chris Hunt, Jenny
Johnson, Ian Burton, Douglas Clark, Ryl Lovell, Stuart Hoskins, Edward
Boaden Thomas, William Oxley, Nicholas Johnson, Charles Hobday, and
Lucinda Carey. My thanks to all of them.

The publisher gratefully acknowledges financial assistance from
Arts Council England.

CONTENTS

1. Poems 1969-99

Odes

To Dance the Sky	9
Laura and the Fwower	10
Down a Byway	11
Stone Circles: Stanton Drew	12
Mutations	13
Clarity and Sanity	14
This Land Sours All	15
On a Winter's Day	16
Evening-still the light	17
Up on the Fells of Yesteryear	18
With my Mother at Brown's Folly	19
It was on a Day of White Frost	20
Signs	21
For my Brother at a Dark Time	22
Burnham Beeches	23
The Light	24
Ode for an English Millennium	25
Black	27
Dark View	28

Fictions

Methuselah and the Parson	29
Sir Philip in Heaven	30
Artorius Dux Bellorum	33
Seth Hurley, Old	35
The General	37
Clarissa Harrison	39
Mrs James	41
The Job	43

Symphonies

Oracle to Pilgrim	46
Asides from Hell	49

Love Songs   51
Symphony One   54
Symphony Two   56
Symphony Three   58
Elegy at the Beginning of Spring   61
The Island   63
Towards the West   67

Conversations
Letter to Charles Hobday   88
At Towyn   90

2.New Poems 2003-2005

Marona   92
Elegy   116
A Horatian Ode   117
When the Great Armada Came   119
The Invaders   120
Pa and the Woman of Good Family   121
Guinevere and Lancelot   122
A Peak in Darien   124
The Heretic   127
The Prophecy   128
The Dragon Smith   129
At Berry Head   130
For Charles   131
The Tune   132
The Track   133
The Stream   134
Hylas   135
The Horn   136
My Love's Walk on Walls Hill   138
Zeus   139
By The Wharfe Towards Sicklinghall   140
The Cove   141
At Wells Cathedral   142
For My Mother   143

To the memory of

Fred Hill (1881-1964)

Jean W. Beake, née Hill (1918-2002)

Frank J. C. Beake (1915-1977)

Charles H. Hobday (1917-2005)

To Dance the Sky

Transient
Tissue of that
Painting the still-eyed wizard
First created

Veil-blue
Dancing the sky
— By whose shimmer the solid
Pink, grey

Sapphire
— Green have meaning
In which the luxuriant and austere
Have made a union

To revere
— Given the courage
To animate the soul's being
And distill the unsinging

Essence
Of song, treading
Unseeably with mental calm
The vivid horizons

Of
The seers, where reigned
Deepest peace, wild self battle
And continual growth.

Laura and the Fwower

Baba stands firm in the road.
                    Baba is most displeased.
Baba considers
            her once despised pushchair
far from mean
            now it's broken down.

Certainly
        you can't complain.

It's a lot
        to expect her
to go a mile
            for what may be
for the second day running
                        a fruitless journey
to get it.

            "Would she like a flower"
says Hazel.
            Baba smiles.
"Fwower" she says
            and toddles forward
very elegant
            in her white betasselled bonnet
and her blue coat
            smiling.

Quite likely
        she'll tear the 'Fwower' to shreds
but to a baby
        that is joy.

Down a Byway

Grey, wooden hut with greeny-blotched, v-shaped tarpaulin roof

Overhung by tall, faintly purple trees, shedding autumn leaves

Where the lane dived deep to a tiny leaf-choked stream

Seemingly abandoned as the once black morris-minor body

Rusting away beside it or the cast off oil drums

The door flapping: peered in: the wind struts

Among straws: night scaffold: decapitation

Hungry . . . most forgotten, so many . . . you might

Be forgiven for thinking the wind in the trees lament.

Stone Circles: Stanton Drew, 1975

pastel-green tufted by orange and brown

great knotted stones as wood to the touch

some upright some fallen

one as a lion leaping

in the background bare great trees

and under them piled logs

and brighter green of meadows in Spring sun

the orange of ploughland

smooth trees

grey-brown with trace of yellow

and the modern nursery and evergreen plantation

the rocks like amiable dead oaks

wandered pennine cousins

indifferent to the electric fence, cow droppings

as the woman we paid to come in

to the curiosity of strangers

in stones her ancestors broke

Mutations

In the marble palace silence is all
The king a shadow upon the wall
The queen in the dragon's claws
And the lion padding on bloodied paws

The staircase floats between blue and black
The white forms come and they never turn back
The clock shall soon strike midnight
And the whole earth shiver under white

White as dense as harsh as marble
White as dark as brute as Hell
But the clock strikes one and black wraps round
Each living form its flesh has found

The queen awakes with her king's arm round
Lion and dragon on the wall sleep sound

Clarity and Sanity

Clarity and Sanity
Black witch sisters of Inanity
Were strolling up the street
When dancing they met
Naked and mud-bestained
Hounds snapping at her feet
Truth that dark indefinite.

They said "She must be helped
To wear our clothes of clarity,
Of sanity and safety;
Be helped to stroll cheerily
In comfort and respectability"
So they chased off the hounds;
And they took her in hand

And they washed her and dressed her
And they had her hair done;
And they married her and wasted her
Upon a loveless home.
But one day they came to call on her:
And her grown daughters denied her
And spat upon her crucifiers

And went and danced through the streets
Bare and young and proud:
Till the hounds of Orthodoxy
came to terrify
And the sisters ran to Mother
Weary and most bitter
Haunted by the memory
Of the first victory of Inanity

This Land Sours All

This land sours all:
Let us go down into deep water

Age-old body of this battered realm
Mutates to a mass grave:
Let us go down into deep water

To free the prince of grief:
Fastbound in deep water

Find the ultimate substance of joy:
Washed pure by clear water

Go down into deep water,
The fruits of our land sour:
Go down into deep water

On a Winter's Day

Such a pure blue winter's day a bit like now
    When frost makes the earth hard and glittering
Light shivers on the lichened green walls and boughs
    And the brown leaves hang down like thin foil
I so utterly tired might as well been dead
    England entangled in order's hydra
Too many desiring their deserved limelight
    Yet I walked by the farms and churches
The fields and bright brooks of ageless Somerset
    Aware of the old squires and their dames
If mouldering remains both their marriages and their
    Loves both those that were sane and those that
Were utterly insane those that helped their rough
    Peasants and those that made their lives dark
And I felt a thawing but so very faint
    Everything seeming too bright and stark
But when I came to the graveyard isle of a
    Small village mother goose was hidden
In the shade of its base protecting her young
    With the dark of man's death and at this
Wise ignorance of a simple bird every song
    that is not man's seemed to glimmer round.

Evening-still the Light

Evening-still the light on the summer green of the hedge

    And on the corrugated iron and breezeblock

Of our neighbour's shed beside it, and our neighbour's

    Head keeps bobbing in sight through the shed door

And his head is oddly separate from his blue shirt

    Beneath, which could be out of that patch

Of blue eternity through the door on the other side of the shed

    Which leads only to the allotment

But my brain insists it is a symbol

    Of not quite hope.

Up on the Fells of Yesteryear

Up on the fells of yesteryear
    The white snows gleam to kill,
And only the bumbling sheep of vision
    Have survival's will.

They are buried deep in that snow,
    The drifts of explanation,
And whether they are dug out alive
    Depends on our dedication.

But we mustn't expect such unwordables
    To give an exposition.
They'll be off when they're warm and fed
    To pasture about with passion

Through tempest, precipice and bog
    The fells' free menace,
And leave us with prewordable life
    We don't know if we can take.

But best finally to have the truth
    Though unwordable
Than live just in the named and known
    The dying and acceptable.

With My Mother at Brown's Folly

They lay here fifty years ago in
The tower's shadow, on a bare moonlit ridge.
   But who can lie down as lovers forever?
Fifty years on bushes and trees have grown round
   The tower, now locked against the young.
Yet young love has lasted through war, and children
   And death (and what else?) till it lights
A single self near the final uncertain end.

It Was on a Day of White Frost

It was on a day of white frost like this that I pranced
   through the fields towards the river.
A robin was perched on the catkins singing.
   There I paused and listened.
I knew this was what I had come for, and not
   the river's shifty hugeness. So I
listened till the frost entered into my feet
   and my nostrils and throat grew too sore
and then returned to where we lived, which even
   now I could take you into each
room of, though it is all of thirty years since
   we left it for a place where the frost
could not craze the windows past the art of man.

Signs

The Romans to resolve
their death-grapple with Hannibal

sent a fair part of their cabinet
half the known world

to fetch a chancy god
from Asia Minor

When I was pruning
the Reverend Goodman's apple trees

nostalgic for a love
that shall not be repeated

an apple on a twig
brushed me with new beginnings

Somewhere beyond hopelessness
the two connect

For My Brother at a Dark Time

The Godsmith of Nihil
is at the atom's core.

How should we cry against the evil
    that buds in ourselves.

My brother would climb the damson tree
    towards the mothering sky

and gather the purple fruit
    with joy, but his jokes

were of the shitten earth,
    and now his mind has broken.

Teach me in these days of uncaring
    to bend like the wheat in the wind

and turn away from me such gales
    as beat even wheat to the ground.

Burnham Beeches

When the winds blow at Burnham Beeches
  and remove the gold leaves from the trees
there will still be that terrible quiet

and the sound of the fall of single leaves
  as loud and final as anything military
in the adjoining regions of our minds.

The Light

The road divides. Her heart-light flickers on.
  Down which road? It is too uncertain.

A distant light, which might be just the moon
  catches trees along the steep way down.

Another flickers in and out
  as on some hidden lane a tractor thrusts its snout.

But where's the light for which I've searched
  every hour without end for over thirty years?

I think I see it sometimes beyond a boulder
  in the grey moor spaces of the inner mind.

I think I see it sometimes in the brittle day
  but everytime I approach it has gone away.

Perhaps if I follow some skywinding bird
  I will find the true point on the card.

Perhaps I grasp where I should find,
  or am I merely man who cannot see his end?

Surely her presence chimed once with mine,
  but since that day I cannot find the tune.

Sin with age makes us all cynical
  and our flesh grows brittle.

But still I reach for her, cannot escape
  the distant beckoning light.

Ode for an English Millennium

The patient tide of whose heart
  is the murmur of our sea
moves inutterably in the stark
    crystal of eternity

and shifts the fallible iniquity
  into a bad-eyed dream
for the posterity that shall be
    different from all we've known or been.

The essence of our material pride
  waxed wild in Hereward
after the arrow brushed the King's helmet aside
    and stone of old churches was overturned.

The poet sang beauty in a London dawn
  though love-hurt himself, and knowing corruption gnawed
the vital organs of a humorous nation.
  I stand as it were on an onanous shore

seared by the sensible doing of little things
  the return of the poor
the insidious niceness of commercial wrong
    blank indifference to past or future.

Send us some inner outlaw
  send us some dream of love
not little things through a magic door
    nor Eros as brother to War

but a mental wood where men may find
  a place of faith against the dark
sure enough to roar with the boughs in a high wind
    and forget the thorny wastes and the sun burning

and when Spring comes with its tide of despair
   and there are seeds impossibly to rear
let us speak of Alfred, broken in war,
   or of a young princess for whom the block was near.

Black

There is a shifting of sand under the feet,
And birds with delicate steps
Make patterns like stars, walking calmly
At no great distance. Great rocks
Perch one on another, islands of
Mutual support, that did not run
With the water, or disintegrate beneath its power,
But stayed, at least for a while,
And in their defiance are uncouth.
And on one of the black islets further out
A black cormorant, another grotesque
In this natural sculpture. And the horison
Has a marking of black, and leading away from it
And its strange legend of clouds
The grey waves do not blink.

Dark View

  Down in the valley
Beyond black rocks and sheep shit and slippery shale
  The orchard trees should be golden with apple
But there is just black fungaed blooms
Hopelessly entangled with maiden grasses
  Who are so slender and tall
  They hide the branches.
There is no future here at all.
  But the sound of the stream goes from somewhere to somewhere
And movement between places is movement in time.
  And though the grey sky hangs like a death about to happen
Small white fractures mark the wind's manipulations
  As it tosses the birds in pursuit of joy
Though mortality is the measure of their movement.

Methuselah and the Parson

He lives in a tent at the end
  of the Tamar Peninsula

beard entangled with seawrack,
  and crusted with shell fish, denying

The Deeds of Men in a sonorous Sumerian,
  much to the consternation of the new Parson,

who, not being sure whether it was
  Latin, Greek, or Russian

alerted the local social work team
  to the possibility of subversion.

"But", they assured him,
  "It's only Methuselah.

A bit tatty, but he's
  been here since the Flood.

And, if you'd been here since the Flood,
  we doubt if you'd look as good.

And the embarrassment of an enquiry
  is something we would rather avoid."

So – like the sound of the reeds on a remembered shore –
  Methuselah can still be heard

denying the deeds of the Human
  in a most beautiful Sumerian.

Sir Philip in Heaven

Zutphen – was it '87?
that I plucked Death
                    – that peacock –
and adorned with the feathers
                              my woman
my unbedded one
                    and found it
thirsty work?
              Much the same
in that golden autumn
                        that ended
what we had begun
                    when they fought outnumbered
on the day of Crecy.
                      Always a good excuse is Death
when your mistress is out of sorts
                                  or you want a new one
little considering
                you may get to Heaven
while she is living it up
                        below.

Gloriana has made a conquest
                        of Wolfe Tone and Michael Collins
and
      bribed the guards
to allow galliards.
                Up here
we get our daily exercise
                        but no dancing
and as for having
                to be polite to Burleigh
and Walsingham!
              Franky

is forever hinting
                    perhaps we could grab
St Peter's mitre
                    and get sent below
but it scarcely seems the action
                                        of a gentleman.

Horatio is surprisingly good fun
                                        but
forever moping
                    after Emma Hamilton.
Someone should tell him
                    that sort of woman
is really not forever.

Winston I never know
                    whether to yield to
in silent admiration
                    or to loathe.

He's forever complaining
                                        the brandy isn't up to scratch
and smoking's not allowed
                                        and arguing with Wavell
over old strategy
                    (Big head Monty
got sent below.)
                    Still he has
introduced me
                    to that very pleasant man
John Churchill –
                    so much nicer than in
Swift's lampoons –
                    and he really likes
my poetry
                    (unlike that prig William
Ewart Gladstone

or that other William
-- coal black Pitt)

It's getting a bit crowded
these days but with
this new (alleged)
Gloriana down in the old country
no doubt
the rate of saints
may decrease
(We got rather worried
in the Sixties)

Anyway additions should stop
in the next hundred years
after the Bomb.

Artorius Dux Bellorum

The remnant of sword-clash drifts back as the boat
    Draws nearer Avalon's sacred isle,
And in it the King lies while the birds murmur
    — Close to death, thinking not of the battle
Or the wind in the reeds (or even of the
    Fierce sap of Guanhamara in
Her youth) but of Ambrosius's still eyes
    Against the firelight, when he answered
"So, my Pelagian, you are quitting, too."
    "Yes, my Lord."
              "This comfort of the soul
Will be the end of us all, Artorius."
    "Yes, my Lord, but I must go. It is
A god-given dream."
            "I can't mend your dreams:
Go!" Ambrosius near to tears then.
And next day ceaseless beat of hooves against wind,
    And Ambrosius tall in firelight,
And the wattled cabin in the middle of the wood,
    Clashing in his brain, so he wanted
Death, and took no care against thieves, but none
    Attacked him. And he came by the height
Of the Ridgeway to a settlement of freemen
    That gave him shelter and courtesy.
And he must listen to their empty rumours
    As one not versed in high affairs, and
Felt guilt at seeking his own peace when the
    Winds of chaos blew so near to these.
So he went next morning up the hill to see
    A priest there of the old religion
— Wanting sense, feeling any holy man
    Would do, but found nothing holy
In that fool's crooked smile.

And walked on the hill
Glancing at the Ridgeway (and the isle
Of Avalon sticking out of the grey reeds).
And he thought Britain might well be held
By a few cavalry perched on this hillfort
In this ridgeway. But he ignored it,
And rode into oblivion of years, to
Learn hard peace in a hermit's cabin,
Till there came old comrades, seeking a leader
For a land the Saxons had broken.

Seth Hurley, Old

The wind rushes through the grass.
He spits and considers the sheep in the fold.
Will not folk be sorted to sheep and goats at the last?
And they have forgot that he is still up here.
He has no debts to any man.
His land is small – but his – as it was his father's.
It will not be his son's nor daughter's neither
seeing he has neither daughter, son, nor woman.
No one may want it – poor land at the best,
though it bred such as beat down a King.
Still the Lawyers can sort it.
Let them make it matter, if it matters
    when he is gone over the river to sing psalms,
or maybe to the fires of the Devil, which he glimpses – mornings
    – but he has his doubts that he might like that
– which must be a bit like a battle
    – something to brag on
– even when someone else did the winning
    – provided you don't think on the wounding.
Quick despatch to the further places
    that was most like a sudden voyage overseas
– as many comrades took when old Noll was gone,
    and no one more to keep the King from his Kingdom.
But the screaming, and the groaning, and the slow ghosting
    – that was bad, better not thought on –
but had to be heard if you wanted plunder
    and being young and poor he had,
for which may the Lord have mercy.
    But those wild spelling Irish creatures
a slow noose and a long dance was best for them,
    and their papistry, and their magics.
But now he is here – up on his father's moor –
    holding a few stones against fox, murrain and the wind

till cold, or the will of the Lord, lay him down
    and he die slow.
Will they note him absent at his yearly market
    and come up?
Must be much how Black Tom felt that winter
    when Newcastle had the North,
and no man but Black Tom ud've thought about winning.
    He could have changed his coat.
Plenty did, and little enough shame.
    But Black Tom and his Dad they bore up
and led old Newcastle with his genteel ways
    such a dance by true soldiering
(of which that Lord knew but little) as prevented the King
    from winning, when the winning ought-av been easy,
and thence Naseby Field, and the fall of an axe,
    which showed that Kings
go under the Laws of England.
    And that, considering all, might
at the last be worth all the grief came after,
    this smelling like sheep, this wind.

The General

He who had been Lord General of the Parliament of England,
  Broken one king and helped restore another,
By the mutiny of his bones was confined to a chair,
  And the shadows of Old Age came across his face
  And he refought the former wars in his mind.
"I have written something in justification of what I did
  And put it in the great chest, and told various people
Where it is hid, and no doubt in time some English Livy
  May give to it the eloquence it lacks.
But in my heart I return to these matters again and again.
  We came to Charles Stuart at York that bright day in June
When Yorkshire had been summoned to doff its hats.
It would have cost him nothing to have listened to our petition
  Which was offered in all loyalty
In knowledge of how affliction had fallen on our Northern counties
  But because we criticised him he took us to be not of his party
So we had to follow him round, and turn our loyalty into a
                                          demonstration.
In the end I ran forward and thrust the paper on his saddle bow
  From which of course he tossed it off again.
And after that, because he chose it, Yorkshiremen trying desperately
  To avoid having to fight each other,
To which I and my Father, knowing it must come were unwillingly
                                          averse.
And when the storm of War finally burst
  You rapidly discovered the true neutrals
Who changed their party with each hint of rain.
  But why was I so certain?
Oliver conceived he had a duty from God
  But to me nothing very much was certain
Except that Charles Stuart meant to break the old custom of England.
  Richelieu had been doing the same in France
And it had been done long ago in Spain.
  Having to discuss one's actions with one's subjects

Must seem a waste of time to Kings, and even Oliver
  When Lord Protector, suffered from something of the same.
But I like a man who meets your reason with his own.
  There was that chap Winstanley, refusing to doff his cap
To a general with the best cavalry in Europe at his back,
But he reminded me of my dalesmen
  Who were heroes in our forlorn bewintered cause
But were known to vanish into an ale house
  In the middle of an overhot retreat.
So I went back to London, and said as much to the Council of State.
  But there are dark rocks about Menston
And over towards Almscliffe, and I grew up
  Seeing the moor about them
Which is neither pleasant nor christian
  And fills me with a dreadful exhilaration
In the presense of destruction
  But also makes you aware
    Of the sheer pleasure
Of staying alive in an impossible situation.
Odd you may say in a man who has looked after stained glass
  And preserved ancient records
  And always been in favour of good government
But it has kept me going all the same."

Clarissa Harrison

The face was like a skull beginning to happen,
But the clothes were still immaculate, and the makeup discreet.
She had a cloak on that day, which added a touch of the romantic,
Which given her known history was unnecessary,
But possibly meant her old bones felt the cold.
She flirted amiably with me who was a young man,
Though it was well known her main taste was for women.
She wanted (to my embarrassment) to talk about painting:
"Do you know what a shock Sergeant was to me once?
I had never seen such graceful tonality in a painting.
Yes, laugh young man, for who remembers Sergeant now,
But he was what I needed at the time.
Later I began to question the burden of reality,
Which is gone as soon as seen,
And I simplified my pictures to the verge of pattern.
This was about the time of my marriage
About which young man I expect you know far too much.
My husband was inclined to say and write too much.
It was perhaps a mea culpa for his previous arrogance.
But the division in my mind at least
Was one summer camping with friends. Marilyn was there.
I expect that you know about her,
Or do you? She gets missed out of most of the books.
She had a weakness for early morning bathing,
And persuaded me, who am a late riser, to go along.
I became fascinated by the extraordinary complexity of a simple
surface
Gazing, half asleep, at that pond while she swam.
A young farm worker surprised us once, and she hid
For obvious reasons, and I tucked her clothes in my basket
And went on with my drawing. Artemis might well have appeared
And had her vengeance on that youth
– As indeed occurs in my much later painting. But he was a pleasant
Enough boy, and did not know on what he was intruding.

Still that scene and that summer were a division in my life
   Though they've never liked those pond abstracts.
Yet I've done them over and over again.
   Too little reality and not quite abstract
An unkind critic once said. But Art to me is a mediation
   Between the forms of the mind and the outer chaos,
Which has its own patterns, but is far too vast
   To seem other than shapeless to us who only see parts.
Don't bother to transcribe that. I've said it
   Elsewhere in several essays no one reads
Except students, who are kept from the inner self
   Of my Art by the need to pretend to be intellectual.
And why have I painted so many nude men?
   Because I love the shape. Look what I have done with them.
No I am not going to tell you about the marriage
   Or Helen, or Sophie. They will no doubt
Speak for themselves as my husband has already done.
   But now, I am getting tired. Perhaps we could stop.
I think it is time for tea, and perhaps whiskey?
   You like whiskey with tea? I think it's adorable.
Afterwards I will show you the pictures I keep for myself.
   They are not particuarly special
But they are things I keep for myself you know.
   Do you have any things like that perhaps?"

Mrs James

I remember James the first – how many years ago is that?
  I went out with him once, and then I finished with him.
I did enjoy doing that: I was a flighty seventeen.
  Yet though I laughed at him I still thought him leonine.
He had such tawny hair . . . and I wanted to be mastered;
  I did not think of freedom or equality
– I enjoyed turning him down, time after time.
  I always meant to give in, eventually,
but he found another girl I did not even know.
  I hope she deserved such ferocious loyalty.
But why should I think of him: that was such a small thing.
  At university I had many men and was lonely.
I was most myself pushing a bike alone on northern moors.
  Where there is nothing is beginning of something.
To be alone with one's ancestors is a mighty thing.
My church was fallen, black-walled cottages they might have lived in
  – those folk I don't even know the names of –
yet something of their solid sense prevents me going mad.
  "All things shall be well and all manner of things shall be well."
They did not say it, but surely they could have said it.
  I was the child of a too early old age.
They were not unkind, but how much did they really understand?
  They had escaped to a bourgeois comfort
via a brave war and a serviceman's degree.
  No doubt he more than earned it, but
he dropped dead at fifty five, and she without him
  is like the skeleton without the flesh on.
Yet loneliness has its reward in this brave new world of ours.
  I worked very hard at my biology, and got
a very good degree, was asked to do a PhD,
  did well at that, and so to an early lectureship.
Yet the yolk of my inner self was barely formed.
  Perhaps better though formed, even if it can be smashed.
He came to know me very slowly James the second did.

41

He ran a course in the History of Science, badly.
I knew so little, and he knew so much we argued constantly.
  I teased him all the time, and he snapped back.
He knew all the facts of history, but had little feeling for them.
  I knew some facts of biology, and understood them less.
Eventually we fell in love (enemies make sometimes peace)
  and to the consternation of our friends we married.
Many worlds we formed to pass in our days' debates,
  and in our nights how many hydra's heads were slain?
The torches lit our days and we were wiser for them.
  But he needed a world to call his own.
I would not give him the room to grow: I was frightened.
  I went to bed with lesser men, and he grinned and bore it.
I only did it to get his attention, and he could not give it.
  He was writing a book from his love's fullness.
I did not understand that: I must have plucked his heart out, bit by bit.
  When each bit was plucked he left me and lived alone.
Why has divorce never come; we so rarely meet?
  And now I have a good job in London, which I loathe.
I hope my students think I am competent and kind.
  I try to listen to the lonely unformed ones.
I know my colleagues think my days of successful research over.
  The real creative thing dies in little more than ten years they say,
and for me that's come too soon to leave a lasting name.
  But some day, when sex has slipped away
like a skin off a snake, I will return to the fells of the north
  and live alone in a rebuilt cottage,
and I will talk to the young of the elusive things
  no one tells them, and the old will call me a witch.
But for now let me grip to dark stone. There are those essays to mark.

The Job

I was called out unexpectedly about
  eleven in the morning, just too late to
be offered a drink, and was asked not to wait

for their architect in the afternoon
  but to dig at the back beside the french windows
and find the old sewer underneath their lawn

and house, which they were quite sure must be smelling.
  For myself I thought it unlikely.
What sane builder would risk a house collapsing

into the remains of something old? But they pay me,
  so I get out my tools, and begin to dig.
Grass and good soil, which came out easily.

But then it was clay – quite dry, and then soggy.
  Now that's hard, when it goes and gets soggy. But
they pay me, so I go on perseveringly.

And they don't come out offering a cup of tea
  but asking if I have found it yet.
And I tell them I can't find anything smelly.

And they look at me oddly in all that wet
  and tell me they're nearly sick with the stench.
And me I can't begin to understand that.

There's no smell there, I think, let alone a stench.
  Anyhow I do get down to flowing water
– and quite a lot of it – full of fish, maybe tench

though how any fish should come to such
  a place I do not know, and they all had
something strange to their mouths. Still it is all work.

So I start to broaden out my hole to find
   this sewer under the house they're going on
about. And that of course is much easier said

than done. But then there's a real complication.
   This water with all the fish in does not run
underneath their house as they think, but is coming down

from what's hidden under those mounds shaped like creatures
   at the top of the hill. Must be some spring hid there.
You wouldn't build on top of a hill with no water.

But I've never worked out what is hid under there.
   It's altogether the wrong shape for a farm.
Strange thing is they applied when I was younger

to close the footpath down past their house from the mounds
   as if their Sixties brick might be discoloured.
But they were turned down, and we walk there on Sundays.

Anyway I told them it straight, and I had to get quite firm
   when they said I did not know my job, and
ought to go on, and that I must be getting warm.

People! Well I told them it was no use, and
   I'd prefer cash. Then they got in a bit
of a tizz and said they'd only got old

money in the house! I ask you! What did that
   mean! Perhaps it was me, and I didn't hear them right.
Anyhow I took a cheque. I did suggest

I filled the hole in, but they said that could wait.
   No doubt they meant for the man who came after.
But they must have got the same from the architect

for they moved out sharpish, and no one knew where.
They gave no drinks, and spoke to no one unless forced;
and why were they old, yet never seemed older?

Oracle to Pilgrim

Cross three rivers
to gain the girl
robed in glitter
of snow in the lovely hills
where no Sun shines
and when the Tyrant
       steals
her away
follow her
through the dark
forest the stir
of strange beings
the
whirr of wings
unseen
until you gain the silent
plain
where all is barren
and only the wind
calls

its dust remorselessly
the same
brutal pain

and then
in death's domain
       imagine your
love
as she was

and a dragon with its tail
will strike you
down

and then smelt you in its flame

but
you
shall arise

and daffodils
shall bloom
but she shall be absent

and a second shall come
small
and innocuous looking
to demand you be dumb
since you disturb
his peace
and when you refuse
he will turn you to dust
and you will lie still
till again the daffodils
bloom and you arise though she is still absent
and a third shall come invisible
and strike you with
emptiness and you dissolve utterly

and the daffodils
shall return and you shall not
watch them then
but come two

new born you and she

and return
by the forest
many mocking

till
as you enter
the hills
you blood stirs

hearing
the beat of
the Tyrant's
drums
the calls of his trumpets
in the distance

the Sun now shining and
the snows gone
his return can be
no triumph

Asides From Hell

I stride
over Earth bronzen
and desirous my
great
      phallus erect: in
      fair guise
I take the queens from wisdom
slake myself
then lead
      them
            to the block and
      direct the fall of the axe
through the necks of their kingdoms
      then I turn
to the kings
beat them
fuck them as women
hopeless burn them and their
peace plans and then

I turn to the kingdom's members
to keep the young women
from bearing fuck them
as men

to keep the young
men away from
            their real self's strength make
them hang themselves or
drive them
      to a loveless
cynicism
      and
      the old

I fill with tremulous negatives
and the young
I riddle with bewitching expectations

it is only after
you can tell me
by the waste
        and then
it's too late: I've passed

Faith's brother gone mad
with his preaching.

Lovesongs

1

You descend like a river
  and become the tides of the sea
and the midnights of your morning
  are the beginning of me

But you hide in strange faces
  that do not know what you mean
and you leave them to dishonour
  the something you have been

2

How should I dance
  now my love lies crumpled
in the maypole-earth

a ladder thrust up
  desperately
out of the trench

3

I am very very tired.
  My soul is on the wind.
I wander through great skies

except these are my mind.
  My soul is always lost.
My love is yet to find.

A little kindness in the dark
  and the light must sear again.
The tree roots now despair.

4
The wind gathers
  in the tree tops.

The moon
  is the snow of us

5
I – like a whale –
  – like a porpoise –
in your sea

when all your waters
  dried away
was suddenly

shivering
  on the grey beach
and dry!

6
"Will she come on the winds of the South
  or the gales of the North?"

But she has gone, my love is gone
  and all lust for life to continue.

The wind must find us and break us
  and then perhaps sun will show.

But who knows at moonless midnight
  whether the sun will come out again?

7

There were dubious islands and a singing heart
  white birds and a faking sky.

None but ill loves now
  and nothing but loneliness of self.

"Come: Singer of Heaven".
  But the tune is forgotten.

Symphony One

Need the mountain because we need the mountain
because the mountain needs us so rend it with
your faith and out of it carve your sacred stones

but don't let the pastel shade deceive. Lurking in
Hate's morass lies the murderous one. Spring him
forth. Yet rather perhaps its Hate lingering

close to Love: both consume. Who's this dancing?
Black they're masked. Black suits, green-spotted. They've shot me.
In the name of the Proletariat. In

the name of the Third Reich passionate shot me
the nameless clowns. Do you see the field of the
shadow, where stir at night all those prejudice

-murdered every class and kind of man, un
-done their doing. The crazy still full moon. All
day, all night I feel its pull. Where are they gone

those birds of light? Moon's guns range now does not pall
but grows more. The birds slink away, their hearts faint:
oil of unfaith cumbers them. Now the Moon will

win. The range of its gunnery grows. Too late
for . . . undone . . . but what . . . a wind of the mountain and
the heather stirs, but, I am bone-numbed: it's too late.

Elegance of unhate. We beat you for your good.
Strangers to truth perpetuate hate. Yet the wind
shall fleece them. It drops. It falls. Tunes are formed.

Growing infinite Time alone can explain,
only Time."Ha ha ha. Death's dancers. Behind
our black masks lurks Death. White bones. White bones, Earth's
                                                        bones

which you never dared to look on."But, the wind,
again, the wind. It must drop; but, it steadies
and the sea's natal rhythms sing. Cities find

their end; Death holds in sway everything man makes,
yet the wind and the water surge, outdo Death.
Stalactite of Jupiter, dust of Mars, lake

of unknown planet, dance dear, dance, oh dance with
the wind and the ocean. These are the children
of the mountain, where Love and Hate are close kin.

Symphony Two

By the glass limpid waters of the Waters of Parable
by the green moss the old dragon yawned, sighing that he knew
no reason why they should survive -- this too gusty young crew
his children, running always from the deepest down soul needs,
avoiding self by tending the sores of the oak trees. Mutable

yet unwilling to admit that years must bring their youth down
to creaking time-beset bone and slowly addling brain.
And he smiled at the Waters of Parable, the moist green
moss . . . bitter their singing of love foredone, their wild longing
for salt maidens of the ocean -- wickedly making down

their menfolk to be bronzen thoughts of the deep sea waves
sharp swords to their own hands troublous from the spirits of the
haughty gods, perambulant in the high heaven in their peaceful
pinks, blues, greens, and most wild darker reds, blacks and purples
. . . Why had HE scattered the dew of his deepest love to save?

There to lie for the old dragon to lap it all up
unthinking; and the brood he so sprung lacked even true will.
Though weary they would not devour their father -- too total.
. . . Most weary he would sleep. "Untrue, your love, compassion
only for yourselves" -- bitter the oak trees, quite fed up

in the way of long invalids. And the young dragons turned
in scorn to a maiden of the ocean. In her they thought
to surely find, real love, if scornful, steely wrought.
But she could only rule. Her neck so they cracked, those gentle
young dragons: in anguish to destruction the oak trees they ripped

from the ground. There was stillness till the gods lifted up
the ocean maidens, and the maidens their men: the bronze
sea waves swept upon the land, crushing all with their tons.
The green mosses, Waters of Parable, fled under earth and grieved.
The dragons, young shrieking, old one smiling, fled to the top

of a great hill. "HE began all this" cried the old dragon
"Now let HIM end it": flew asunder, fell as a dew, to bear
peace to waters and green moss. His sons, bound now to bear
the burdens of the ocean maidens, found almost pleasure;
waters, green moss, were self complete: far off HE smiles unseen.

Symphony Three

1

Creation's nothingness would rend;
but, I'd glory in the silence,
marvel at the forms – dinosaur's
sixty mile an hour pounding, or
the amoeba's one cell: growth
in all things, but nothingness: so
hopeless: mortal weep for and
praise all dead in the shifting ground.

2

I hear the walkers moving with scrunch of gravel
I see the walkers coming, gay with the visage of skeletons

they go as to a funeral or a feast
lithe with madness

I finger the outlaw's hand
he says he is of the old religion
I neither one nor the other
and the stream murmurs to the uncaring oak

one day something will happen

3

Through the trembling light the child shadows
Over the brown land. I hear his sighs
Through the wind's batt'ring capricious blows:
"Why must I shadow here never to burrow

To the dark cool caverns of my forbears
– Through embracing dank soil, to those jeweled
Wonders they built in bygone calm eras?"
But the wind and the rain smile, mild

Contemptuous: "The child will remain here, while
We, through many seasons, wear him right away".
And, indeed, he will see nothing blissful

But, only grief, till his uncertain end. Yet
The meaning in him, shall outdure the play
of Nature, and in Eternity's scale, find weight.

4
Out of the sheep-fleeced mist
The wind's own child spoke up:
"Wither greed's carnivorous seethings
From out of creature's wild lips.

Let storm the midnight's passion
But cool the noon's high heat.
Despair of Life's abysm
Despair of Faith's fate

But laugh with my mother of the gale
Dance with my father of tears:
For in them is the durable way
Steadfast beyond false accord.

For your world is a maze of cold particles
Moving remorseless through form:
Out of your fingers' seven year dooms
Change, spun on the mangle-fingered Fate's loom.

But I am a wraith of your imagining
– To live in your verse, or to die;
And seeing mankind is a fingertip to eternity,
What of yourself – and, of me?"

5
Like a chattering child
In the creaturesome dark,
I would stay close to the light

— Uncertain, of what may lie
In the place of eternity
. . . White-boned valley,

Where soon I must take up
My burden, till the dawn disclose
That calm, green plain, full

-Flocked with serene dreams of my
Completed people – before, and, to come.

Elegy at the Beginning of Spring

The heather was so still, ominous with the
  Storm's calm coming, and nothing moving.
If we had approached Hell's lost shadows and heard
  The baying of the hound and the clink
Of the cash surely it would have been like that.
  But we saw Fylingdales' ghostly domes,
And turned down into the heaven-lighted peace
  Of the valleys, upon our right road.
And Steve too in Brighton wandered past midnight
  By the wild lights of the seafront and
Lay down before the insurging ocean
  As one craving the darkness only.
And at that small castle the shadows seemed to rise
  – Master killed by his wife and her lover –
And the rope and ashes littering Tyburn.
  And giants are the walls of Raglan
Where Fairfax forced a breach, and all but ended
  The War between King and Parliament.
And Parliament had then to justify all
  The ossification of good men, and
The use of genius to poor ends, but couldn't.
  And I see the dark one in the depth
Of lunar stillness, his attendants flitting
  About in fitting sobriety;
But outside carousel whips around, and they
  Make mockery about the chariot
Of the too sure overseer. But at Kielder
  At Kielder the pebbles all ground in fate
To the tune of the diamantine light and
  All the faiths in my life seemed renewed.
But all knights must return from their quest and see
  New dragons uprisen in their lands.
Did not Fairfax see the fruits of civil war
  All squandered for a new tyranny?

Yet though arthritis, stone and lost faith bore down
　　He arose at the height of winter
And restored the cause of a balanced realm. And too
　　When the ninety years of your Gran were
Returned to the earth, and you stood by the grave
　　I walked our six-month son by great trees,
Each a dark thicket of centuries, and thought
　　Of that stone coffin, its small white bones
Graham's plough upturned, a five year old child
　　— Dark grief to unknown faces of un
-fulfilment. And there was a sudden breath of
　　Wind, and a flittering of swallows.

The Island

"Memories, memories of what?" asked those eyes
Too luminous for a human skull.
"Memories, memories of what?" asked those fingers
Twisted with arthritis or misadventure.

"Why stranger, what should you know of the ways of truth
Who never followed your heart's truth I think,
Never put convenience into a sack
And cast it in a pond with your parents' intentions?"

"Madame your story is widely reported.
At least give me the facts as they were."
"I care nothing for the fantasies of men about women
Or of women about men.

The facts of our journey were such as they were
– The ending dark, myself the survivor.
As to the imaginations of lewd men
Because we were bright-eyed and soft-fleshed

And a brotherhood wholly female I do not care.
As to the contempt of prurient women
– Set in their ways, manipulating men,
Abominable to children –

Let me tell you I was never one of them
And I despise their contempt . . .
And anyway who would believe the ending . . .
We in the white ship with the white sail

Much grimed, salt caked, smelling most unfemale,
Exultant at the danger of the storm,
'Will of God' we called it, driving us on
To our pilgrim's end, still unnamed,

Better friends in danger than before on land
(And yet several wept or bitched)
And suddenly blue sky, white clouds, even a little sun
So that some talked of miracle.

And behold it rose, it seemed, out of the waters
An island, so you could see the falling
Of waves remaining out of the trees.Was it,
You say, perhaps hidden by the storm?

Perhaps, but I was there, prefer the miracle.
And miracle it was to young girls sea-beset.
We grounded on the beach, had strength – just –
To haul our craft up, washed in fresh springs

Plucked at fresh fruits – such fruits – and ate
And lay and drowsed in the warmth of the sun.
Waking at night in the fullness of the moon
We heard a tune of strange dancing

Measure to make young feet tap, but
No dance that we had ever heard.
And giggling and merry we followed that sound
Forgetful of austerities

Through woods of oak, ash, elm – much as this island's –
But there were no hostile creatures as here
– Nothing, not even mouse-scamper, owl hoot, but
A condition of exultation.

In a wide clearing, too wide for nature,
And yet no sign of human kind,
We met the music of the dance, seemingly
All made by the branches of trees

Each tree moved by some power
Out of its rooting into motion.
And the young ones we did not disdain to be
Prickled by. One even danced with a holly

But myself I chose a hazel, and was still a little scratched.
And so through the night: exhaustion on exhaustion:
All slept. I waking found that island sinking.
I cried as time permitted, but they slept.

I ran to the ship, found it floating on the tide,
Swam to it through cold snakes of ocean,
Servitors of Death, clutching at me, clutching.
Held desperately a while to a rope

Knew I must clamber aboard, struggled, strove,
Tumbled finally on planks, lay while the boat
Was swept on, watched while the lightning
Sheeted round the rigging, knew I must sink.

Was blown finally upon this coast of black rocks
Which the orange lichen paints on a
Summer's day, but not then, not then,
Was dragged out by evil men

Out for plunder, finding only a virgin
Had their way with her, finding
Her barren, a cost without fruit, threw
Her out again, till I came you see

To this well they call holy, by the side of an oak,
　　In need of a custodian.
And so I have performed for wine and bread
　　Lawless acts of prophecy

Occasionally the rites of the courtesan
　　To men (not many) I looked happily on.
And every night I dream that this oak
　　Will tell me the fate of my companions.

Do they dance with the great trees
　　Happy at their prickings?
Or do they lie under the ocean, their bones
　　The toys of deathless beings?

But I dream they rise with the island
　　And go down at its going,
And I am close Sir to believing that's true,
　　Though under grey skies hope has no place.

So Sir: your story. Do you wish to stay the night?
　　The robbers and the wolves are restless at night".
But he looked at her eyes, fiercer than life
　　And he rode away into his truth.

Towards the West

Part One

"Music is a mathematical consideration"
    so utters our knight, most contritely
following a ridge above a stream and looking
    at a sky that is black, grey and blue, and battered

by the wind. Branches of the beeches along the way
    creak a music not of Heaven.
He remembers his lady's fingers on her lute
    – like a flight of small birds her tunes –

and knows her desires are not large or far reaching.
    Another mistress must be looked for soon;
but for now this image still sustains
    even as a subject for violation.

Leaves are slippery under the hooves
    and almost like clouds the jaws of the pass.
Is it that lion of the true transfiguration
    or the dragon of former magics

which he sought to consider as the Dark One's works
    but whose volutions he begins to feel
must be before those becomings in the soil
    which worm, beetle, bone know.

* * *

Midnight by a stream, whose molten black water
    might be the ultimate metal,
the moon a perfect round in a sky of annihilation
    which is the beginning of creation.

He longs at first for the warmth of anyone,
  but is chiefly constrained to pee.
He considers the violations of his friend Francis the monk,
  but a monk must pee and fart.

Has brother Francis ever considered
  the motions of the spider in its weaving,
that are done not for money or god
  but to trap the living flesh?

Is it a sin in this tiny spider
  to eat of the flesh of the insect ape,
to drink of the blood of the insect child,
  disembowel the woman of the kind?

But here sleep takes him and he finds himself
  in a garden full of thorns,
that once were young maidens, and hot for child,
  and now are full of unkindness.

* * *

The awakening at midnight, the endless birdchatter
  (worse than women discussing their rivals
with insinuation rather than anger)
  the distant glimmer of the bars of Heaven

this surely is no beginning to charity
  – merely a day of aloneness, and riding towards
the pass, where hovering from time to time
  possibilities, always possibilities.

* * *

"You arouse me" she had said "To be with you
    forever, and not a queen
to a man who is no man. You have done what I asked.
    Get off. Plead your quest. Well

if you can't then you must think of something
    for me dear, unless you want me dead."
And he had gone, weary as in a dream
    of great waters closing over

the eye of the silent king, in his own eye
    the blood dripping through the bandage on the thigh.

                    ★ ★ ★

About the middle of that day (the sun was behind cloud)
    he came upon maidens and young men
making a bonfire of the leaves of the autumn
    looking they said to summon past spirits

to give hope that the Spring should return.
    "Why" he enquired "Are you dressed in green?"
"Because" they said "although we must grieve
    all things return, if not for us."

"But you" he said "have all the youth of the sun.
    You are the heat we rise upon.
I am who am neither old, nor indeed young
    go to the West, always towards that pass

confident that from you shall arise new heat.
    I have seen love miskindled and betrayed,
I have seen Love that woke only in dreams
    but still I continue towards the West."

                    ★ ★ ★

Eyes, eyes like swords in a sheath
   that may be watching from the trees
– as once with the army of the king
   in the forest of the Idlings.

Cowards! Why would they not come into sight
   – at least unleash an arrow –
but all was still except for footfall
   too quiet for knight in armour to hear

and once a fox trotted in front of the column
   glancing at the king's majesty
without fear,and then loping on,
   and birdsong unnaturally slight.

The king had not declared he had put by conquest,
   but the column never re-entered
that wood, and those that came out
   questioned their knighthood.

And now that old fear of having no purpose
   strikes on a still afternoon
in quiet woods with gentle sun
   by a translucid stream.

* * *

To lounge in the sun with armour off,
   drinking deep of the nectar of Apollo,
and forgetting the pains of that other son
   whose blood redeemed the winter's woe

and forgives the casual spearings of the spring,
   this is to know the reality
such as it must be to drink of that cup
   of heartred, unseen and unseeable

whose power lies through the dark high rocks
   of the pass somewhere further to the west,
which if he did not sometimes see
   like clouds of storm

he would think was another pretence
   of that false reader of signs
who walks plump by the side of the king,
   and is said to spend time with the queen.

                     ★ ★ ★

Ambling along the river valley he met
   with messengers sent by the king
their surcoats fierce with an imprint of lions
   demanding why he was taking so long.

Had he stopped too long as a guest of the nuns?
   The Mother Superior had hinted as much.
They could not speak of maidenheads broken,
   but there are other ways of doing the same.

And had he not heard of the great dragon hunt:
   Sir Archibald slain and the hunters disarrayed?
One more spear might have decided the issue
   and another church set up to Saint Michael.

He did not speak of his sympathy for dragons,
   the peacefulness of their fires unless aroused,
nor yet of holy converse with the beautiful and fair,
   and unusual things done at midnight.

He did speak gravely of his utter dismay
   that one on a quest should be called on for dragons.
Were there not a hundred dragon-skilled as he?
   And so the messengers pursed lips and went.

* * *

At fords knights hang basins to get a good joust,
   but he objects to having his brains beaten out,
So he never bangs upon such basins,
   but avoids all fords like that

even at the cost of swimming the stream.
   Doing this today he thinks of baptism
– Christ and John the Baptist at Holy Jordan
   and the voice that uttered out of the clouds.

That voice then had not spoken for centuries
   and has not ever spoken since.
The fullness of water is the beginning of things.
   The Lord uttered it wisely before time was.

And now today he enters gladly the bath of wisdom
   whereby he shall be cleansed
of the human animal's ill doings,
   and be fit for that cup of heart red.

* * *

Waking up in the full light of morning
   it has been raining the shepherd says
(who gave up a bed for this flea-ridden knight)
   and rain will come although it is bright.

Perhaps the lord would care to stay? He looks
   at his dream-driven guest
with that pity the practical and treacherous feel
   for men whose minds are just a little astray.

The knight proceeds by the compass of instinct,
   swimming the river where none should have dared,
leading his horse through misted water meadows
   mud and trees to the edge of the moor.

Following an old track (high over the moor)
   are those armed men that he sees on the other side?
Who travel the path the shepherd told him
   – sent by a king to judge by the ensigns.

An escort to the pass that none will go through?,
   conceivably protection against wolves or thieves?
Or murderers, sent by that monarch of the bleeding thigh
   to avenge the adultery of a few summer evenings?

Or recall (conceivably) from that other king, his own master,
   at some whim of the wizard who enthralls the queen?
He takes off his surcoat, covers his shield
   and takes out the favour from his helm.

He lets it fall in a pool of mud.
   The time of her is done.
He must go on alone, unhindered.
   Chaste music only sings in the pass.

* * *

The river grows narrower, faster, towards the pass.
   The heather is passing out of its purple.
Soon will be winter, and blackness
   – as in the time of his first beginning . . .

the peat hovel on the edge of such a moor,
   the few brief people who cared for such a child,
till the fever took all but him,
   who was given good herbs by a wandering man.

73

He was no knight whatever in his origin,
   so why did they choose him
to go through the pass for the cup of heart red.
   A moorland child perhaps with natal sense

for such country, or had better knights died
   in decent oblivion?
Such information is so hard to come by
   and perhaps better not known.

He returns to the mathematics of rock and cloud.
   Black versus white does not equal grey.
The white shapes of the devil are very many.
   The true black is so very rare.

Part Two

Scree scattered with black boulders
   marks the first beginning,
dark lichened cliffs to either side,
   and the air heavy, stale.

The horse – apprehensive – requires the spur,
   and himself tense at some predator
nibbling his mind, speaks only of dreams,
   and here and there scatters of bones

which might be sheep, goat, knight. Probably
   not knight, for the scrolls show none entered here,
nor would he have done, but for that magician
   who has, it is said, the ear of the queen.

Yet having come he continues on.
   Return is shame, outlawry, the rope;
Present a tune made out of numbers
   – a deathly thread to dance upon

but a thread, and one that may not snap.
   But slowly he moves, glancing side to side,
sees only rocks with the faces of demons,
   but he knows that they are rocks.

            ★ ★ ★

Night coming on, and the pass all blackness
   he pauses, considers where to lie down,
noticed a slight opening under the cliff
   – perhaps the horde place of a dragon

but that smell was wholly absent,
   and in any case he enjoyed conversation with dragons
– their jokes of great learning, their flame of creation
   out of the wordlessness long before Man.

A place opened full of strange shapes.
   Thought it at first the entrance to Hell,
and candle revealed twisting shadows, but proved just rock
   rubbish, the bones of some human

which he buried with correct courtesy
   (not wishing for the haunt of its ghost)
then laid out his cloak – and his few provisions –
   and made ready for sleep.

           ★ ★ ★

Walked in a place whose floor was of green
   and purple the pyramids scattered around

and there came fair young girls
   virgo intacta
with the face and the fangs of a pitiless snake
   and kissed each one a pyramid

so it turned to a youth hirsute as a goat.
   And they made such a dance
of twinings and buttings, such anger, such laughter
   such entries to places not normally used

and green was the corn in the field
   and green the anger of the wind
and stern the mountains over
   and oppressive their cloudbeard.

           ★ ★ ★

Awoke next dawning, teased, worried.
  Found the horse under Death's rigor.
Carried such things as a man may carry,
  stumbled to whatever end.

So similar – grey rock to grey rock he wondered – time to time –
  if he had turned, was going backwards;
but still he continued on a day of fierce rain,
  wind absent, hail down-battering

till, around noon, he found another shelter
  – inside it rubbish that might burn –
which he managed with difficulty
  . – body shaky, teeth chattery –

fell suddenly asleep, bread and cheese still in hand.
  And this time there cavorted
– grown fat, slack-buttocked – that queen he had loved
  with her king of the bleeding thigh

grown suddenly young, eager for lust
  – though the blood still streamed from his thigh –
They beckoning to him (so it seemed)
  but he watched as one frozen to unmeaning

and they laughed at him for his discourtesy
  said that he disdained a true discovery
– that all true love has no outward seeming,
  then tickled his nose with a feather.

★ ★ ★

Awoke – the first motion of the sun
  since entering the pass,
but fitful, without any real heat
  – just a flower ghost in the clouds –

but a sign – as after that flood –
    whether of the Ark Man or Deucalion
(whether the wrath of the Lord came twice
    or different poets told the same differently)

and there was even the sight of an arrow of birds
    threading westward (into what realm?)
– not quite the dove with the twig in its beak,
    but a sign of something to one alone.

★ ★ ★

Suddenly he pauses, looks at the lichen
    and sees bright sunlight on it,
and finds it wonderful this world of many beings
    is remote to man as this pass.

And he took off his boots, and bared his feet,
    and washed his sores in a pool.
Cool as a girl's breast the water, and he felt whole
    almost. But this could not be the end

for all said the pass led into the west
    to the cup of heart red:
of which no man knew the true property,
    but so many desired. But he was now hungry.

★ ★ ★

Hunger stalked him in his joyfulness
    – hunger like a tide, driving.
Was Death the water of that tide?
    But Death he feared no longer.

It was dread of Time that drove him on
    at a greater speed than a well-fed man
but sleep became more necessary
    and he lay and slept in the sun.

* * *

One with a staff, a striding rock
    (birth-stone to fanged flyers)
and glares with an eye of winter blue
    and snarls as one who knows everything.

And this our knight would have followed to the end,
    but a wraith of blue light
made the time-fast free, led into waters
    endless, indivisible

and sweet as air to the taste:
    creatures there were without any flesh
– being, all being, and out of any time;
    but this must all come to an end.

* * *

He strode it seemed suddenly upon dry land
    – land sweet-natured for the planting,
and spade and cup both only in wood,
    and no dark one, no quake god to harm –

but this he knew was vision beyond attainment;
    and he woke weeping, ravenous,
resolved to push on to whatever end
    (though dubious if this pass would end).

* * *

Stumbled up the pass with the dusk light over,
   body creaking in its joints,
the last bread gone, weak.
   One it seemed gave him a staff

– his own and forever – if only he would go on;
   but laughter came on him,
and he knew that anyway he must die,
   and suddenly – and abruptly – lay down to blackness.

* * *

Woke dreamless to a sun of great radiance
   the whole pass a coal about to burn.
And surprised not to be quite yet dead
   creaked round a corner, and saw

a wide plain – greener in its grass
   than the music of the spring –
and clouds of rain – sufficient and adequate –
   and elderly dragons (puffed up with importance)

demanding to know the reason for this intrusion
   by a scarecrow, come from the sinful and human
– whence none had come since Time first evaded,
   though a guard had been fixed at early eternity.

He said he was just a poor simple knight
   – come in search of the cup of heart red –
but presently in need of food, drink and a bed.
   But they looked at him uneasily

gave him a bed in a middling dungeon
   with a stew with good herbs and a better wine.
But the door was guarded very closely,
   and instructions were asked of the hierarchy.

Part Three

The colour of slate – the table –, and grey as dust
   the three creatures – there, not there
(perhaps with beaks like voracious vultures;
   perhaps frog-slimy, or beetle-black).

They asked (they seemed to know) why he had come here?
   Why did he trample the preserve of sinful dreamings?
And just to tell those of flesh that sin is chosen,
   but not by man, and unmaking rattles

in the dreams of the smiling infant
   like peas in a pod;
and sentience is a dance to a brittle end
   and death in full brainhood the best.

But he said to them emptily (confused by their assumptions)
   that he had feared too much to be afraid,
and found himself back in his ill-lit dungeon
   (and the mailed feet on the stones).

* * *

One came to him with a great clamour of locks
   – a dragon in blue, striped dark and light –
demanding to know what was his claim
   to enter this realm no knight ever entered.

His glance attached to the poised quill of the secretary
   the knight could give no answer
– beyond commands clearly given by a king,
   and unnacountable compulsion.

And this he realized as the scene was switched
   to a circle of aloneness
was not the answer they intended
   – however much the truth.

★ ★ ★

It seemed then suddenly that this circle of grey
   was on top of a hill where nothing might grow,
and there came a young girl (like his first lover)
   to immolate herself that the land might have growth.

But none could she find to draw blood from her willingly.
   And he who would have helped her
at cost of eternal pain
   knew himself beyond her sight.

And he wished that he might be drawn skywards as cloud
   to rain down the blood that might save her young shaping.
But she continued to dance a step of futility
   lacking the life to take away her own.

★ ★ ★

Suddenly news beyond all expectation:
   a pass from on high
– great grumbling of dragons officious as ever –
   but a pass come suddenly.

So he set out treading lightly on air
   (his escort of song birds)
and the air warm scented as after love yielded,
   and all beginnings to somewhere.

★ ★ ★

Cloudshapes of anguish cloud idyllic sky voyage:
    sense of brothers, who were one (however dissonant)
relationships divided to the sword's push,
    and daydreams as of some woman

– perhaps that very queen he once doted on –.
    So he finds in this journey of reverie
the very seed of her devilment,
    which dark arts should have wrought

but seem in his eye like an outcome of lusts
    and the egging on of a king
(who may or may not be his own master
    but is too careful of his honour) . . .

Or is this all angst to spoil his delight?
    The green copses are singing
shades of all making, and the boisterous mating calls
    enliven an easy passage.

★ ★ ★

Sudden the great wind – causing descent
    toward the bank of a brown river –
hastening away in total unmerriment
    the joys of all lovers whatever.

He pauses, a wraith dismayed on the bank,
    seeking a ford to this fearsome being,
tending a case but hardly believed in,
    longing again for the touch of the real.

But the ghosts of past memories spite him,
    remind him of lusts that were barely conceived,
and shrivel him up at wise paths sensibly taken,
    good causes shewdly not fought on.

But came that first breath of all beginning
    and renewed him to the rock of new singing:
so the water of that river covered and cleansed.
    And surely he became as his first spring

and green growth in abundance filled him out.
    and still at centre his first meaning
– at which he flew again through air
    with haughty escort of eagles.

* * *

Landed safely in meadows fit to lounge in,
    and the brooks babbled like half dreams at sleep-edge,
and warmth as of a truer sun
    than ever shone this earth upon.

And he lay, all mazed, with no forming,
    aware of the shadow upon the field,
which was of a castle – grey, oracular
    as if offered truths none living might know.

But for the time expanded the wraith of his meaning,
    and gathered from root of all beginning,
and made his sense from matters precedent
    to the first memoried coming.

* * *

Rock of all rock, and before rock what?
    The eagles over never knew
how this wraith gathered sense past thought
    while they warded away his ill seemings

till gradually he rose, and looked at that castle,
   and put on new flesh of that further place,
and strolled towards that gateway, eagerly
   expecting – he knew not what.

Passed first great sentries, dog-headed in stone,
   then in the courtyard unformable flowers asleep
– fold of rich velvets, that concealed new beginnings,
   having drunk of oblivion.

But these he put not on, scorning to be
   other than as at first his sense told him;
but walked steadily to the second wall
   of glass that distorted all

so the face of his being was wholly unmale.
   But he knew to consider the self as it was,
so came quickly to a place of great ruin,
   where once was the treasury of All

– now looted, and spilled on the ground
   such small jewels as still remained.
And at this he cried for all sentient,
   and turned a little nearer to nothing.

★ ★ ★

Entered on the spiral of nothing next
   that returned always to beginning;
and this continued as surely as annually
   the bee comes and goes.

And this he continued with all the pure strength
   of one who cannot go any further,
and therefore must stay in the same place.
   And this continued forwards and back

always glimpsing the illogical real
    – men bold into badness
(women as bad) and creatures he knew not
    – could never quite touch their being –

plaiting strange air of stranger places
    with an appearance of ugliness
worse than Man's, or rising with infinite
    rareness into great beauties

uncommon as his kind's. But as he came
    more and more, to feel as all
– and yet to be separate, he began again
    to become perhaps something.

* * *

Suddenly, that cup of heart red
    – all liquor of all beginning before
all beginning, siezing all sense
    out of nothing and all –

and he looks on it, and knows he will go back,
    must, though the guise of flesh has no comfort,
and they will warp his true being,
    and of all the true journeying will be no remembering.

* * *

Alone the young woman, since her lover chops wood
    and the child's coming is abrupt;
and the ferns of her bed know flood of life water
    and the hovel leaks.

And the future is sere for any here born,
    and the ague shall take her
before the child has seen ten summers,
    and before many days the child as well.

And one shall come wanderingly, half mazed
    and discover a boy near to death;
and out of his healing make new beginning,
    and steer him to intellect in this wildnerness

till time come to take him to the Court
    (always eager for knights to slaughter its nightmares)
but out of this one shall come the evasion
    – the singing out of all beginning.

Written, Bath 4-14 May 1992.
Revised, Bath 4-31 March 1993.

Letter to Charles Hobday

Charles, sprung of Sussex stock,
Whose verse matures like your native oak
— Green sapling longer than most,
True, but with age grown druid subtle
Not least in that you've kept your youth's first rage
Against the dark dividers of this realm,
Whether those magistrates that sabred free speech at Peterloo,
Or Mosley, Baldwin and that crew
That rose demoniac-dithery out of young men's
Ill-spilled blood, or now Maggie,
Witch of high conviction and wild flight,
Brewing in her cauldron the wrong spell
And calling it right, yet always with a twinkle
In your eye at the more laughable policies
Of your own party (or any other)
It seems time to end this sentence
(Which is long by English, if not Latin standards)
And wish you a happy birthday.
Yet the oak I am forgetting is a magic tree.
By oak, ash and thorn so Puck
Leads the children down to Merlin's isle of Gramarye
— The place of strange gods of name unknown
(Or are they known?) that fascinate your fay side,
That animist who lurks dancing
Behind your fierce anti-jehovism,
And tempts your audenary muse
by dark and dragon-howling moors
That were legend in the time of your loved Arthur.
And though War stalks our race,
And our industry is mugged by a government
That claims to reclaim it, and
England has too many grown cynical
Or idealist, yet out of
That ancient dream and faith

We may survive, who knows, prosper?
At least, if the world will let us
We poets can rebuild a little the slipping foundations
Of our consciousness. The English phoenix
Never before failed. Why should it now?
And doubtless you will add
A little laughter will help it on its way.
Anyhow, a merry birthday Charles.

September 9th 1980

At Towyn

Be quiet, be quiet, be quiet! No need to rush or to hurry!
    Last morning here at Towyn, last of the holiday,
Though the end of interminable illness is somehow hard work,
    And even sitting quietly by a gas fire is altogether an effort,
Yet I have walked the quiet hillside road out of Abergynolwen
    By gorse in the first gold of Spring, that outshines later mintings,
And come out into the flat land (calm under the mass of the hills)
    And smiled at first lambs – barely able to stand – and the delighted
Distraction of their mothers. I clambered on the single central
    Island of rock that Llewellyn made his castle
(Though it passed from the Welsh after a brief while) and studied
    Harsh and crumbling distances of hills, which were once
The heart of an implacable resistance. Two days later
    Coming up the other side of the same valley I communed
With T'ang poets, and noticed strange crooks stuck into stone
    As if the land waits for shepherds, and was haunted
By an image, which came I do not know from where, of a young
    Woman in a gown of green. At Porthmadog on the day between
I left the venal tourisms of the town and walked along
    The estuary, and noticed two birds (too indistinct to name)
Flying in low and fast as if to get under some natural radar,
    And a man on a water scooter made a great deal of noise
That seemed only to emphasise how little of Man's there was.
That day (and yesterday) I went in trains at the meeting
    Of the sea and land. And it struck me how much we go
Not by the banks of the Styx, but beside some endless
    Sea of renewal. My faith I think would lead me
In a black ship with gold-haired maids in green, endlessly
    And not in some weary boat across a marshy stream
With the possibility of a dispute about change!
    But last night, I'm glad to say, serious thoughts got put by.
I went to the cinema and saw Towyn's gay and raucous youth
    Rather than the film. They squawked with the elemental joy
Of birds in the sky, which send to me, at my return

To the dull and income-scratching world of home.
I want to take from these three months of illness
  And these few days of holiday a something of joy.
But such things are in the hands of gods, not men.
Nevertheless bring sense to my life again.

May 1999

Marona

Book One

Prologue

And it is written of Marona
    daughter of Maron

Lady of Confederation
    Mistress of the islands

Queen in War
    beyond expectation

subtle in peace
    and healer of contention

that knowing a few chance songs
    she had uttered in youth

were widely known
    and not always correctly written down

and that she was credited
    with victories that were not her own

she had this parchment made
    with her few songs

and her memories of that time
    when young and alone

she was defenceless in the time of evil
    and still came home

later to lead us to those things
    that are of record and well known.

I

I came first as a hostage
    to the imperial city,
and my bowels were liquid with fear,

knowing the reputation of our lord the King,
    and that I was to be a companion
to his terrible daughters

who we feared worse
    than his captains,
who ravaged our neighbours

and were now at our borders
    – worse almost
than his executioners,

though they made
    a spectacle of respectable
honourable families

who had ruled justly and long
    – and their retainers
by the hundred.

But our galleys
    crept into the bay
out of a still windless sea

under a tiger sun,
    and I saw the great white buildings
in the fierce light

soaring towards Heaven,
    and I knew
we would survive,

and the realm of my father
    would not
be put to the sword,

or my priestess mother
    to the collar,
or the rest of us

to the axe;
    and this tyranny
would have its day,

but why
    this was
I cannot say.

2

I remember the presentation
    to the High King
of course:

the slow motion forward
    through silks and bright breastplates
– and the wild colours

of the decorations and orders
    each in that court wore
– like a dog's collar!

And the way that
    – not that unobtrusively –
we were guarded

on each side by real warriors
   (devoted no doubt
to their warrior lord,

whose campaigns had brought to the old Confederacy
   the order and union
that the military love).

And I recall
   the blank face
of the High King

-- so like looking at a mask
   under his great red-jewelled helmet,
for a moment

I thought it was a mask.
   But I barely recall
the sentiments

offered, and given
   on both sides
in accordance with custom.

What I remember most
   is the aloneness
after the abrupt dismissal

of my escort,
   my standing
on some landing

by the statue
   of a great eared elephant,
and some woman

(of no great importance)
   coming to take me
to a small room

on the fringe
   of the daughters' apartments,
and her saying

something like
   I should remember
to stay out of sight

and never seek
   to be talked to,
and who knows

I might survive
   – though we both knew
few hostages did.

And I looked out
   of the great window,
and saw that the sea

was royal blue,
   and the stones
of that evil city

shone like some vision
   of Heaven
– which was grotesque.

And I remembered my acquaintance
   of the wood,
and thought that perhaps

one day this might all
    turn round if he
and I lived.

But I saw little chance
    of any of that,
and I wept

without tears, for I thought
    that tears
might be dangerous.

3

To come and to go
    more or less
 as you want

to be fed well
    (better than at home)
and at the high table

if at the bottom end
    and to have
little asked of one:

not too bad
    you would have thought
for a quiet young woman.

But I dreamt of the woods
    in all their variety
of leaves

and I thought of my father and mother
    – and my not
very admirable sister,

above all perhaps
    of my young men,
who loved me

at a distance,
    and whose laughter
and worship

was the air
    I breathed.
And here I was no one

a mere hostage,
    whose death
would be ordered

for a whim,
    or for sound
political reasons

sooner or later.
    It was wise
not to be seen with me.

The eldest daughter, Festa
    occasionally
sent for me.

But to be liked
    by Festa
was a dangerous thing

and I responded
    as little
as possible.

But loneliness,
      if you survive it,
is a great education.

There are things about
      the interactions
of mind and body

no book can teach.
      You learn to survive,
and to dream.

And always
      at the back of my mind
that strange conversation

in my beloved woods
      with a man who seemed
a little mad.

And from time to time
      strange poems
came into my head.

4

She Remembers the Meeting in the Wood

Lady Marona, daughter of Maron
   – slender as alder, bright as the birch –
riding your palfrey, harness bells jingling

faithful retainers in surcoats,
      bright in their raiment,
brighter than is wise in the forest

have you noticed how the birds are uneasy
    because you intrude in their space,
you and perhaps certain others.

Perhaps your retainers should lead you
    into a place of at least partial safety
– if that does not offend against your dignity.

Otherwise crow and vulture will peck
    before long at the eyes and orifices
of these jolly young men

and who knows you might find yourself in a dungeon
    with no attendants to bathe and dress you
– or – at the very least a hostage

in diplomatic splendour, waiting an answer
    from your embarrassed father,
who has already considerable anxieties.

5

Marona on the Beach

You are different, Fishermen.
    I am happy to get my skirts wet

among your boats, nets and huts
    while your kids play tricks

round your brusque women,
    who are overworked with your coming and going

and the gutting of fish.
    I raise my eyes

to the light
   that shimmers through the grey sky

and then look down to the radiance on the dark waters.
   Though you go in the shadow of great storms

you move among beauty.
   I wish I could go with you.

6

Marona in the Park

The carriages and carts press forward
   along the great avenue that borders the sea.

The ghosts of leaves dance about them visibly
   and (in imagination) ghosts of human beings.

In the park by the avenue a little tree
   moves with the wind – a sculpture in its way

much better than the great bronze monstrosity
   that is meant for our Lord the King

on which the ridiculous scavenging gulls
   shit with impunity.

But then *they* come from the sea. Oh look
   at the sea – how it roars!

Oh summon Sea your tempests, beyond any in memory
   and wash this place away!

7

The Dream

My Princess! My Lady Festa! Sore on my soul
    – like the feel of ice

which will never melt,
    here where the very walls are of fear.

The body of a beautiful woman such as yours
    (such as mine certainly is not!)

ought to have a certain presence
    – even under full court robes,

but yours as you sit in your royal chair
    never seems to move. It was even more so

in my dream last night. There was no matter to your head,
    just an outline. And through that shape

the hounds in that bloody hunt tapestry behind your chair
    raged baying, and I ran through a wood

hampered by my skirts, knew soon they would reach me
    but suddenly (it was a dream)

were leading me to a clearing
    – and the moon was bright.

In that light they had human heads
    or their leader did, and he said

"Seed of our future
    wax fertile in wisdom!"

And I woke. The gods it seem
    mock at me in my misery.

8

Marona's Song of Despair

Stone! stone! stone!
    – it rubs against my nose

and there is water flowing in.
    Soon I must drown

which is easier;
    – or be ground.

There is no escape.

9

One of those interviews
    with the Princess Festa
– meant kindly, perhaps.

"It is time
    for the Autumn Hunt.
You have not seen

our woods and hills.
    Being our guest
you are of course

confined to the City,
    where, incidentally,
I gather

you like the sea,
    and are not seen
as often as I would have expected

in the Palace.
    We keep an eye on you
– for your own safety

of course.
    I would be happy
for you to come

on the great hunt,
    as my guest.
I will provide you

with the clothes,
    as you would expect
– you will look quite elegant –

and a horse,
    and men
to keep an eye on you

if the boar
    gets too near.
Being a guest

we will not of course
    trouble you
with the accoutrements

of the hunt, though no doubt
    you know
how to use a bow

– do you? But it is
    of course
wrong to trouble

a guest with having
    to kill
the prey.

We have men
    to do
that sort of thing."

I was fearful
    that I might
be "the prey"

though I comforted myself
    that my Father
was sure

to be up to date
    with his tribute
and did not seem

to be suspected
    of anything.
Or was he?

But there again people around
    the Princess Festa
disappeared for no

very apparent reason
    and something inside me said
"She likes to kill."

The Hunt Departs

The great gate opens in the great grey wall
And the bright-robed column sweeps through:

Guards in bright scarlet with sword, spear and bow,
And solitary after them on a great roan stallion

the High King with a boar spear,
And then his daughters

the three gold-haired princesses
smiling cheerfully, cracking jokes

– would anyone have imagined them
such mundane creatures of evil

in their well cut hunting gowns
– a quiver on their back

a bow on their saddle –
but a guard of course to each side;

and then the huntsmen, with the hounds
– soon to rush like fire

through meadows and woods,
but now almost under control,

and then the rest of us
– not a dagger between us –

and then the burnished armour of the rearguard
and the bright spears.

Still it was something to leave the city
    after days that seemed like years

and see wavering trees and not the ocean
    or huge walls of stone

and observe red cattle with flies buzzing
    and reach woods and smell leaves

and be where trees keep something of themselves
    and animals and birds flicker by

that know nothing of high kings.

II

Hope, of course I had hope.
    Out in woods
such as I grew up in

Perhaps, just perhaps
    some mad boar might charge
and remove High King, Princesses and all.

I would have been a willing victim.
    But, as happens
on such occasions, nothing occurred.

But after that we returned
    and the fresh woodland air lingered
and melted away

the ice of doing nothing.
    Not the ice of fear
you understand.

It had never entered my head
    that I could do anything.
I was here to die,

and must be remembered
    as one
who did it bravely.

Then I wondered
    if I could
slip up the great hall

– something wrong with my dinner knife
    perhaps, a female in a muddle –
cut that bearded royal throat

before a guard noticed,
    perhaps even
the softer wind pipes

of the princesses. But the guards
    were too efficient.
And to die with nothing achieved

very slowly and very publicly
    was not my intention.
Then I thought

of the fisherfolk, and escape by sea.
    They let me go on the beach
(though they watched me)

but because I was watched
    the fisherfolk
smiled nicely

as one does at someone
      you know
has something

which may be catching,
      and is possibly fatal,
and hardly ever talked to me

12

After the hunt,
      after my realization
I could do nothing

bad dreams and despair
      glare back
at me still.

I see
      those two hostages
suffer as I might have done:

a brother, a sister
      – I did not know them –
their father ruled the mountains

in the Island of Winds
      and was not pliable to demands.
So first I heard

they were held in some dungeon.
      then that they were on bread and water.
Finally, that the patience

of the High King was over
      – and no doubt with it
their usefulness.

Certainly, they were brought out
   on to a wooden platform
(they never bothered to take it down)

outside the royal prison
   in garments filthy
with the mire of the dungeon

– it was always how it was done –
   and made to stand with placards
round their necks

pelted by those
   who shut their eyes
to what the High King did.

And then – how does not matter! –
   they lost their heads
– as I might have done.

I know the boy was pitiful,
   and the girl kept her dignity
– which I could not have done.

But did I see it?
   Was I made to watch it,
or do I just remember

the gossip
   of every common citizen
– and no doubt the pretty girl

who after a fashion
   gave some attention
to my bodily needs

– kinder
    than she need have been –
but she chattered, oh she chattered!

13

An interview with the Princess Festa
    (that faceless face again!):
"We hear some malcontents

over whom your Father claims
    he has no control
elevate you

into what you are not
    – a martyr
to your island's freedom.

Since you are here,
    wholly of your free will,
as an ambassador

from your Father,
    this is of course
a libel

on my Father;
    but I expect
you will write

a letter to your Father
    which he may publish,
making clear, my dear, the truth

about these strange misunderstandings.
    If you do not
it may go hard

with your Father. Mine breathes
   of reparations, of war,
which – for your sake – I would avoid."

Leaving her presence
   I felt the width
of my neck.

14

The Escape

i
Isolation, loneliness and the fear of death
   did not quite destroy me.

The anniversary of my captivity came round
   and it struck me – I had grown.

If and when I came home they would see a woman
   with firm judgements,

not a girl whose ideas veered with the wind.

ii
Day of liberation come unexpectedly as a black sun!
   My little pretty maid came up from the kitchen.

"My lady, they are talking of some fire."
   Which was meant to explain her absence I thought

– Scarcely a matter of great importance.
   chattering to young men as usual.

But then another summons from Festa:
   "There is no cause for alarm, but there has been a conflagration

that has consumed a large part of the town.
   As a precaution we are arranging for the evacuation of our
                                            guests. Go

and gather your things
   and make your own way

to the main gate of the citadel
   where there will be an escort."

"Why no escort there?"
   I asked my maid.

"If you just walk out there are not
   that many guards."

"What will you say?"
   "That I lost you."

I saw her kicking her pretty legs
   on the gallows.

"My lady, just go." I went.
   I do not know what happened to her.

iii
Would it have been better
   to have stayed?

Often guilt at leaving her
   outweighs joy at my own escape.

Anyway I have seen nothing like
   that walk through the city.

unknown anger of gods
    smoke rolling

and dust
    – so hot!

no sense of rank
    – all unkempt

unkempt, and moving as if mad.
    All were a little mad.

And where the fire had died down
    the map of my mind was torn

streets – gone.
    Disappeared – the terrible city.

I followed others and hoped.

Staggered too near the flames,
    and lurched away.

Earth likely to open
    and gather us in.

iv
Breeze shifted the smoke.
    The sea was royal blue

and absurdly still.
    I was by myself.

The beach was awash with white ash
    – shingle, sand

and pools slimy with it.
    Sea – so still, and the light of the sun bright

jewels no jeweller ever made.
    The ships from the harbour

The long lean galleys
    and the broadbeamed merchantmen

equally unsure, whether to come in to shore
    and risk the ash,

or stand off, and hope
    a few would swim to them.

And quite unbelievably

my father's green serpent ensign
    limp from a stern rail.

By a pure chance they had come,
    knowing their embassy hopeless,

desperate as a drowning man for the surface,
    dreading war, needing peace.

Swam out,
    was hauled in, and they knew me

from a world of youth
    forever gone.

The captain – a young man
    I had flirted with often.

They greeted me as one returned from the dead,
    and set to their oars.

Elegy

Disdain not the valour of young men who go
    to war, knowing the consequence
and return with sordid nightmares in their souls
    having done hard things, that evil
might not flourish, and dark shadows fall.
    And if some revelled in the adventure
and wandered out of their way by the gorges of death
    that was always the right of the young.
And if this death or that was harsh or pointless
    do not talk too easily of waste.

A Horatian Ode on My Son's Visit to New York

Let there be bright stars, and no headwinds,
        And no diversions over Greenland,
And no interventions from Al Qaeda
            For the plane in which my son is carried

From London to New York, and no other ambushes
        Of fate or work. But you know
He must have been a tough old sod – that Montgolfier
            Who ascended in the aether

Without rudder or propeller. And later at the siege
        Of Paris more than one made their escape
by means as perilous as staying down below.
            It must have been a darn sight easier

For Orville and Wilbur: they had at least a rudder! And much
        The same goes for Blériot, crossing the channel
Like a giant Beetle. And Alcock and Brown
            Defied the clinging ice

In a relic of the Great War, traversing the Atlantic
        In a mission more desperate than most even
In that mansucking conflict. And then there's Saturn rockets
            And space shuttles and whatever.

But lovely though it is to ride the sky
        At thirty thousand feet I do sometimes wonder
If Man was meant to do this. Our ancestors thought
            That ships were quite dangerous enough!

And since Einstein and Co. let the atom out
        Weapons of mass destruction gather
– Not to mention nuclear power.
            Like Hercules before too long

We'll be sending a task force to deal with the tyranny beyond
                                        Acheron.
        There's nothing we men won't try.
And in the follow up to that it should be easy
        To enter other dimensions.

But somewhere God (or something similar)
        Will be waiting to laugh at our stupid vanity
And push us over the precipice
        We missed on our way up.

When the Great Armada Came

Now when the Great Armada came
    Drake shrugged his shoulders and said
"If good Queen Bess chooses to be a war monger
    pretending that Philip of Spain
means to extend his dominions into this ancient isle of Britain
    when clearly he is only sending reinforcements to Flanders
to help fight the Dutch, who are anyway a threat to our economic
                                        empire,
    and anyway she has not bothered to pay me for the last three
                                         years
I must make a stand. I will not walk with placards in Whitehall,
    but in a calm manner deliver leaflets for Betterware.
And if Leicester has to die very boringly and heroically at Tilbury,
                                  and his queen
    walks out to suffer the same axe she tendered her cousin of Scots
(though more likely they will only send her to a nunnery)
    I will be able to rest secure in my conscience.

The Invaders

Descending to the kitchen in the middle of the night
    She found a slug on the dishcloth, and a slug on the floor
– Curiously between turds and jewels to the sight,
    Conglomerate of green with something darker.

She wrapped up the invaders in paper napkins,
    And a bag of the latest plastic,
For she did not want to kill them off for making expeditions
    That originated in the nature of their beings.

At the back of her head came pictures of ancient serpents
    Lurking in mud-floored underworlds,
Able to creep into the architecture of our modern places,
    And subvert what is well-made and of this period

Into visions uncomfortable and slippery,
    Lurking in corners unseen,
Waiting for the unwary to put down a foot,
    And endure the ancient infection.

Pa and the Woman of Good Family

Her petticoat rustles, she carries a sketchbook,
    And she is looking for a subject.
She spots this interesting eight year old from the lower classes

And offers half a crown, just to sit on a fallen tree
    Over the stream. Half a crown!
Meat for next week to his Ma

Skimping by on bread and milk
    In a different world to this siren
Who sketched and sketched all that afternoon

Constantly telling him not to move.
    And Pa sat, getting stiffer and stiffer
– But dead keen on that half crown.

And she finishes, and tosses the coin to her collaborator,
    And walks away with a rustle of skirts
– Eager to show off her sketch to those at home

Perhaps even to a future husband,
    Thinking that well worth half a crown
– And such a nice little boy!

No doubt she did not choose to see him fall in the water:
    if she had attempted to be brave and fish him out
Her pretty skirts might have pulled her under.

Guenevere and Lancelot

"There is mud beneath the great beech now it is autumn,
        which makes our game too obvious, and anyway I do not like
to wreck too many gowns, and even Arthur
        asks questions, if still light-heartedly,
about my desire to watch every bird in the palace wood.
        I cannot have you in my chamber.
There is enough gossip to arrest me. A more jealous man
        or one less wrapt in the good of his country
would already have taken notice, but later or sooner
        his enemies, who know I am a bulwark to him,
whatever my feelings for you, will waken him to his injury,
        which will lead inevitably
to death by the lion of judicial fire.No doubt there will be many
                                                                            songs
        about the queen who spoke fairly to her lord
while she wiled away her time in adultery;
        but I would rather live to love you, as long as I am able
and give my lord the wily council of a woman, which is cannier
        than the tempestuous blunderings of councillors.
But this does not mean I do not wish to see you.
        There is a tourney at the castle of the Five Pines
on the Hill of the Four Winds, and Sir Mark its castellan
        understands such things as are between us two,
and was a page at the court of my father, and he would be glad
        to have the true Queen as his tournament's monarch."
"I could escort you, and perhaps perform" said Lancelot
        suddenly aware he was out of practice with his lance.

So Guenevere said one day to her lord, King Arthur
        "Sir Mark of Five Pines on the Hill of Four Winds
requests me to be queen of his tourney. I would gladly
        ask you to come with me, but you are busy.
The Ambassadors of the Princes of Ireland take all your time.
        Adjudicating the boundaries of Ireland could take a thousand
                                                                            years!

And the Prince of Brittany will be with us soon, and only you
    can entertain him. I will ask Lancelot to escort me.
He is not much of a man for politics. He is good company,
    and I am sure would like to participate.'

But King Arthur answered "The ambassadors of the Princes of
                                           Ireland
    do not like my adjudication, and will soon be gone,
and the Prince of Brittany writes to say he is delayed.
    We can ride together to this Tourney.
For once I can see your beauty grace an occasion,
    and perhaps I will break a lance myself.
But Lancelot of course must come. He is most welcome."

"Must I really come" said Lancelot, when he heard that decision
    "I would rather not have done".
"It is his will. We must obey" replied Guenevere
    fearing the fire, and tempted by it.

Yet each man and woman at that tournament
    spoke of the light on the face of Guenevere.

A Peak in Darien

Sparrowhawk over the island: the children have not seen it.
The high hills in the distance are full of shadows:
Clouds like warrior ghosts. Are they brave, or bad and bold?
The sheep anyway survive, not to mention the shepherds.
By a pine tree in Darien a man and a woman.
"Yes, the children call it Darien. Quite poetic don't you think?
Oh you like poetry do you? Well my children are quite keen on it.
Won't last of course. At least I hope it won't.
But still it might help you get on with them. I hope it will.
Wouldn't do them any harm to know a real man.
Father away, and all that. And after that time in London
I think you're pretty real James.
I wouldn't have dragged my children half way across England
or got them risking their necks in an old dinghy
for anyone James. No, not here my love. Its not quite private.
Wait till tonight. I'll have my cap in. Much safer.
I don't want any more of the little dears, and anyway
it would be hard to explain with George in Hongkong.
No wait till tonight. I've got Mr Jackson eating out of my hand.
He will think nothing if I borrow his boat
and slip out to you, imagine I've gone for a dusk paddle
to look at the sunset. Bloody romantic!
Bad as my kids. Titty anyway. Suzie's naughtier.
Needs her bottom smacking!
Won't get it of course being a girl. George would be quite shocked,
though I might get round to it myself one day.
Would do her no harm at all! Silly little cow
– always thinks she knows whats best for everyone.
Don't know how the other kids put up with her!
Still I will have to keep an eye open for their boat.
Can't expect children by themselves to keep to bedtimes,
and would not do to be caught in flagrante by my own offspring,
at least not yet. Anyway I've given George two boys, and rather too
many girls.

I don't see he can complain if I have a fling!
One of his friends tried to warn me he's got a bint in Hongkong,
    but that's his affair as far as I am concerned,
unless of course you and I get beyond a certain point;
    but not many people like us get like that
do they dear. Too public, altogether too public,
    and George might even be mean and take my little horrors,
though I don't think he would. He is not a bad soul is our George.
    Anyway I've never made love in a houseboat James.
What will you do? Put a mattress on the floor? Don't worry about
                        the details!
    I'll help. What women are for!
And James, you really must tell me about Lenin.
    He sounds really quite fascinating. And Trotsky too I imagine!
But I hope you are not too much into communism, dear.
    A little money does help to grease the wheels.
Is that why you are writing a book? Oh not poems James!
    There's nothing ever in that,
though my youngest daughter is still at the silly age they like to
                        recite rhymes!
    Hopefully she will grow out of it soon!
Oh you're not serious James. If it is poems I do hope there is
                    something else as well!
    Still your sister did give me the impression
you have a decent amount of pennies to rub together, the pair of you,
    so perhaps you can indulge it.
It's not as if you are living in the time of Wordsworth.
    He must have made a pretty penny in his day;
but that is a long time ago. But still I am looking forward to tonight.
    As I said I've never made love in a houseboat.
It ought to be different, as long as those kids don't board you
    just as we are really getting going.
If they do I will have my eldest son touching his toes.
    Oh James you surely don't not believe in corporal punishment!
It's the most natural thing in the world, and so effective.
    I don't know. Why do I love you?
You have such odd ideas. Yes I will come love, yes I will, you know
                        I will.

No don't come down to tea at the farmhouse.
They would think it just a bit odd you know,
    and we would neither of us want any gossip, would we?
Till later then love, till later!

The Heretic

The priests say the Drummer dreams in Heaven
    Cadences like moonrays,
Quivering like willows in rain,
    Or sun on lake waters,

That have the indistinction
    Of a square before dawn,
Where indefinable shapes roam
    In a world not the same as our own.

He can reach the individualities of each moment,
    Between dream and waking has no borderline.
His purposeless visions have a completion
    We down here have not lived in.

But we can go out in rough weather,
    And know the joy of a journey achieved.
We can bask in a steady sun
    And let our wayward thoughts run wild.

We can do what was never our intention,
    And find our beginning was really our end.
Even his imagination must be proper and fitting.
    Ours can taste of laughter and darker perversions.

Yet he is our lord, the drummer that dreams in Heaven.
    Our priests spend their lives teaching his conventions.
To rule here I must ascend mountains
    To present my people's petitions

Yet I do not submit to him.

The Prophecy

If there was only one who might be heard
    Above all the clattering inaccuracies.
The mirrors of our immaculately trained wizards
    Are full of smoke and uncertainties

About which they mutter bare audibilities
    – Adumbrations of not too serious surprises,
That will above all demand no unexpected expense
    To cause taxes unspeakably to rise.

If there was only one of them who had seen for real
    The mind's barely perceptible cliff-edging trails
and was unperturbed by the once laughed at tales
    Of crouching evils, that now enter our reality

Then we would advance towards these coming sorrows
    with something approaching committed faces.

The Dragon Smith

Green moss, green moss, black with soot
    and the high rock roof stained
by the craft of this scaled dragon smith
    who fashions with impervious paws
the dreams of the kingdom.
    The place is all odds and ends:
trees from spring, leaves just out,
    roots with no home in mother earth;
song birds raucous with lust;
    bodies – human, feral, of each kind
– flesh that is soft, flesh that is hard,
    waxy as ripe fruit, or tortured
– but always in imagination;
    babies to come, or not to come,
as yet without faces;
    unlikely deeds, sudden creations,
disaster breeding sudden hope;
    tragedy to cleanse the impossible;
impossible beauty: all the craft
    of the Dragon Smith.

At Berry Head

The waters beat at the cliff foot,
    and those much-shaped beings the rocks
take on the aspect of unutterable creatures
    that grow hard with the demands of survival.

Clouds the colour of ink
    waver like a floating island
in the subtle-hued ocean of the heavens,
    and the round white circle of the moon

spreads on the corrugations of the sea
    a light that is improbably golden
on waves that throb and toss and whiten
    to the half globe of the horizon.

For Charles

Alas old friend the winter gales
    have set loose huge ocean rollers
into the bay where the rusting freighter of age

has sought a doubtful refuge.
    It swings on frayed cable
– all that maintains your ancient order.

Soon it will snap and the current seize you and break you
    under the sheer cliffs.
These bits will be tossed around

the local beaches. There lovers walk
    hand in hand – true! But still towards death.
Some – I hope – will catch a glimpse of your name.

The Tune

I hope you no longer hear that tune
    Which is in the first place the tramp of an army
Pushing Youth forward to the punctuation of a bell
    (Though Youth would act anarchistically!)

And then turns to the slow movement of desire
    Before it quickens to the proper directions of adulthood
(As we are led to believe is supposed to happen).
    But my vista turns positively wild:

For a brief while the world is yours to roam
    And things long dreamed of can be seen.
But now is the slow halting march to an uncertain end
    After which you are barely known

To have been on this earth, that is greater than each human being
    And maintains in its seasons our constituents
– Plant, animal, air and water that sustain –
    And contains more knowledge than any of us can

But, where ever you are, and (though I miss you)
    I do imagine sometimes some timeless dimension
(Which my science denies) at least you are beyond
    The insidious music that means my time is taken.

The Track

Grey trunks lean over us
    but the sun bursts through
as if we are in a temple of great columns

and the leaves are jewels
    – each brown, each yellow, each green
multiplied by the light

into so many, many coronals – through which
    we hear: "Though this is the season of autumn
and ours are the colours of that time

and though we will vanish,
    and winter lines of black and grey
replace us, yet our successors

of the Spring and Summer
    will arrive in their time
in epitome of love

which has its seasons
    of fulfillment, and colours
infinite as the ocean,

and its necessary times of withdrawal into dark,
    but if true
returns forever and again.

The Stream

You have brought me back to the bank of the clamorous stream,
                                                    that was present
        At my beginning, and almost washed me away;
But in my bad days was only audible underground:

For the harsh world would have drained and sealed the springs of
                                                    Helicon,
        And put the gracious Muses to useful work, and as
To the ancient knowledge all I could do was conceal it.

But now the old springs are uncapped, and flow fresh
        Before our mutual sight, to co-mingling delight,
Between the tree clad banks rolling rocks in amiable fury;

And here you and I stand, and pause, and draw
        Into parched and longing souls
The still and fertile force of this irrepressible energy.

Hylas

There is a slight mist in the autumn wood,
    And odd shadows shift between the trees,
And there is a stench of rotten leaves and dead
    branches – yes!, but also a scent that goes

With the faint cries (noises anyway) as of some presence
    Which draws the young man
– Whom war attracted, and now has horrified –
    Off the skimpy path to where few else have been

His senses full of the anticipation of the wholly wild.
    He moves so quickly to avoid his doubts.
He seems hooked to some inreeling line.

He is drawn to a pool. In it white water must have always rushed
    Over slowly shifting mosaic of black rock.
He puts a foot in, smiles, steps further, vanishes.

The Horn

There came an owl with a silver lance
    – riding, riding –
Perched on top of a delicate unicorn
    – Saddle of gold with rubies blazing –.

Hung from his shoulder (just ready to blow)
    A silver horn
That could recall the notes that formed Creation
    In the terrible dark before the first dawn.

But little the owl knew the truth about that,
    For he had it from his dad
– Passed down so long the tune was forgotten –
    But nevertheless he was very glad

To have this bright precious horn for his own.
    And from time to time he attempted a tune,
And produced a sound beyond adequate description
    – Unless between a fart and a cow in pain.

But the subtle notes of the mysterious first one
    That put in order such different things,
And made of many a related whole,
    Never entered his honking.

But the unicorn, though much sat upon
    And pricked along with a cruel, cruel beak,
Knew in its soul what that horn had done,
    And listened and longed for the tune.

And by a waterfall there waited a troll
    – A rustic, cudgelling, thieving cully,
That fought the owl, and took his toll
    – lance, saddle and horn back to his hole.

He makes out three notes of the ancient tune.
The head of the unicorn suddenly stirs.
But the owl is away to its brothers
To regain what was always theirs.

My Love's Walk on Walls Hill

My love went for a walk on Walls Hill
    Through the socialising of canines
Clutching a green umbrella
    Because it was terribly windy

And suddenly she and her green umbrella
    Went whoosh on the wind away
To the summit of the sky
    – High! on high! on high!

And right at the top of the weather
    She saw three dragons passing by:
Green, and blue, and grey
    Painting a circle through eternity.

And then the air drained away
    From the green umbrella,
And she fell, down, down, down
    In the winter-grey sea

All the way to the bottom
    To the sand, the weed, and the stone,
Where the great maw of Leviathan
    Scattered the dust of creativity

And she clutched at it eagerly,
    And rose up inexplicably
Through the realm of fishes,
    And left the changeful sea

And found herself suddenly
    In the acrid smell of a shelter
In the rain on Walls' Hill, clutching a broken brolly
    And the dust of creativity.

Zeus

Many a diffident teenager
Succumbed to Zeus' suggestion,
Or was intrigued by a transformation
– As Leda by the Swan.

Lucky girls were everywhere
Pursued with righteousness,
But the number of kids they spawned
Was past all reasonableness.

Zeus had done his dad in,
And battled giants down,
And you cannot vote a tyrant out
For ignoring the manifesto

And when you are the Law
You need not go to court,
So Zeus was here, and Zeus was there
And the girls got all the blame.

The ox-eyed Queen of Heaven scowled,
And summoned harsh chastisements;
But the Lord of Gods is here, is there,
And love of a sort is everywhere.

The Spring is bright, and the corn grows high,
The ocean is fertile and evasive,
Memory is creative in the minds of men,
And new things are on the earth.

By The Wharfe Towards Sicklinghall (circa 1958)

Descended among tall trees – not particularly old,
    Pines planted against the exigences of world wars –
By the green iron bridge over the brown leaping river
    That everyone crossed with a certain sangfroid
In despite of the notice defining the presense of danger
    – A little boy in blue mackintosh and red cap
Seeking, perhaps too eagerly, the horns of outlaw romance
    And the sudden whistle of arrows against the unrighteous.
Approaching sixty, in unreal recollection recall
    The tremor of horses' hooves, and the uneven thump
Of unsprung carriage wheels, but also an odd
    Glinting presense of great creatures
silver-winged keeping watch over the amiable
    Small folk of an imagined earth,
None of which makes much sense to rational men
    – Myself included on my reasonable days;
But the images that flooded unintended in my childish head
    Are firm and growing in my adult years,
And I am glad that there is something
    Beyond the cold exigences of clay.

The Cove

Somewhere there is a cove with blue grey waves lapped in the sun
    And strange birds swooping, and black rocks dry enough to
                                            sit on,
And a man and a woman perched on one.
    They talk – quietly, calmly (in time now gone
Or going to be) wearing (both of them)
    Long robes – striped (the man's) purple and white,
 But hers saffron with a silver hem.
    And on both their faces a great light.
And yet the same faces have all the signs
    Of the terrors and pain of the survivor,
And the robes are stained with salt, and ripped on rocks,
    And their faces are sore, and burnt by the sun.
Why do I think I am witnessing a great power
    By which many dark things may be undone?

At Wells Cathedral

Never mind the toy clock and its sonorous medieval tournaments,
    Or the tombs of ancient bishops

Carved into the skeletons
    That we all become

Or the remnants of Saxon walls
    From a conquered forgotten establishment

Or the glimmers at the back of the mind
    Which may be from those that made offerings at ancient springs

Or the place where the Clergy (reverend and otherwise) conferred,
    Or even that Dean who gave thanks for the ending of Civil Wars:

At Wells Cathedral there is a great quality of light
    And all the joys of silence

For My Mother

Four years (almost) since you left us. Where are you now?
    I often ask myself that question.
But does it matter. The shoots that began in you
    Have inched their way through frozen ground
and now come slowly into flower. No things
    run right forever on this earth,
but the memory of your days, and before them your father's,
    brings a certain graciousness to our lives.

Printed in the United Kingdom
by Lightning Source UK Ltd.
119378UK00003B/46-54

9 780907 562986